# Looking Back at

# Houses and Homes

SCHOOLHOUSE PRESS

**Copyright © 1988 by Schoolhouse Press, Inc.**
**160 Gould Street, Needham**
**Massachusetts 02194**
**ISBN 0-8086-1178-X (hardback)**
**ISBN 0-8086-1185-2 (paperback)**



Author: Anne Mountfield

Editorial planning by AMR

Designed and typeset by The Pen and Ink Book Company Ltd, London

Illustrations by Jane Cheswright and Trevor Ricketts

Picture research by Faith Perkins

Printed in Hong Kong

88/89/90/91/92/93 6 5 4 3 2 1

**Library of Congress Cataloging-in-Publication Data**

Looking back at houses and homes.

Includes index.
Summary: Traces, in text and illustrations, the evolution of houses and their furnishings from prehistory to the present day.
1. Dwellings--History--Juvenile literature.
2. Furniture--History--Juvenile literature.
[1. Dwellings--History. 2. Furniture--History]
I. Schoolhouse Press. II. Title: Houses and homes.
GT172.L66 1988 392'.36'009 87-16524
ISBN 0-8086-1178-X
ISBN 0-8086-1185-2 (pbk.)

## Photographic Credits

*t=top b=bottom l=left r=right*

The author and publishers wish to acknowledg with thanks, the following photographic source 25*r*, 43*t* J Allan Cash, London; 31 BBC Hulton Picture Library, London; 21*r*, 37*b*, 42 (photogra John Bethell) Bridgeman Art Library, London; title page, The British Library, London; 7, 9, 13*l*, 17, 39*l* Douglas Dickins; contents page, 25*l*, 30-3 32-33 Mary Evans Picture Library, London; 1 Fotocolor ENIT, Rome; 32*b* Fotocolor ESIT, Cagliari; 22 Fotomas Index; 5, 36 Sally and Richard Greenhill; 43*b* Robert Harding Photograph Library, London; 6*r*, 28, 40 Michael Holford; 10*l*, 14*l*, and *r*, 21*l*, 29, 34*l*, 39*r* Hutchisc Photograph Library, London; 14 L Murray Robertson; 23*l* (photograph J Gibson), 26-27 (photograph John Bethell, 35 (photograph J Whittaker) National Trust Photograph Library, London; 20, 30 Picturepoint (UK); 18, 23*r*, 27 41 Ann Ronan; 10*r* Sheridan Photograph Library; 34-35 Frank Spooner Pictures; 6*l*, 8, 12, 28-29 Zef (UK)

Cover illustration courtesy of The British Library London

The publishers have made every effort to trace the copyright holders, but if they have inadvertently overlooked any, they will be pleased to make the necessary arrangement at the first opportunity.

**Note to the reader**
In this book there are some words in the text which are printed in **bold** type. This shows that the word is listed in the glossary on page 46. The glossary gives a brief explanation of words which may be new to you.

# Contents

# Introduction

We all have to have a place to live. We have to have a home. Homes are shelters. In cold countries, homes keep people warm and dry. In hot countries, they shade people from the sun. People have to have a safe place to sleep. They also have to have a place to meet their family and friends, and to store the things they own. Our homes are the places where we feel we belong.

## Caves and Shelters

The first people hunted for their food. They gathered plants and berries. They followed wild animals from place to place. They lived in caves, or in huts made of branches or grass. Sometimes, they dug holes in the ground, and covered them with grasses or hides. These shelters were used mostly for sleeping. Fires were lighted outside for cooking and for warmth. These fires also frightened away wild animals.

## Beginning to Build

About 7,000 years ago, people learne how to grow crops. They began to kee animals in herds. They no longer had t hunt. These people were the firs farmers. The animals were their food People began to live in groups and t share their work. In some places, th land did not grow enough food to fee everyone. They had to move on whe their animals had to have fresh grass The people built huts, or they made tent which could be moved around easily Sometimes, they put a fence up aroun the huts and tents to keep everyone saf from an attack. These settlements were called camps.

As people learned more about farming, they began to live in the same place. They did not have to move around. People began to build houses that were more solid. They made tools to help them build. They also learned how to use different materials. They divided their houses into rooms, and added new parts like windows and chimneys.

◀ Lighting fires used to be hard work. Early people had to rub sticks together until they began to burn. Once a fire was burning, the people tried to keep it lit for a long time.

People in ancient Britain lived in small huts of ud and sticks. Roofs were made from grass. nces were used to protect people from wild imals and from enemies.

## Finding Materials

The first builders used the materials for houses that they could find nearby. They could not carry heavy materials from far away. Houses were made of stone or wood. Bricks, made of clay, were also used. Stone and clay were taken from the ground near the buildings. Wood was cut from the forests. In some places, mud and leaves were used.

Today, builders use materials made in factories. These materials can be brought from all over the world very easily. This means that houses in different countries look more alike than they did in the past.

▼ Today, many houses are mass produced. The same materials and designs can be seen in many parts of the world. These houses are in Detroit, Michigan. They are warm, dry and comfortable.

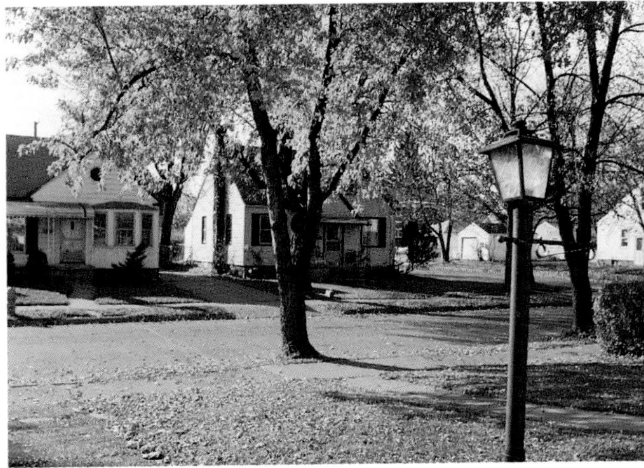

# Places of Safety

People first built homes to keep themselves safe. Danger came from the weather, wild animals, and enemies. Homes were used for shelter and sleeping. People cooked, ate, and worked outside their homes.

## Keeping Cool and Warm

In cold countries, houses kept out the wind, the rain, and the snow. Builders made thick walls and long, sloping roofs. In hot countries, houses had to keep out the sun. Some houses in Spain and Mexico were built into cliffs. The rock kept the houses cool. There were no windows or doors to let the sun in. The entrances to the houses were down ladders from holes in the roofs.

▼ It is very hot in the desert areas of Tunisia in North Africa. Underground houses like these stay cool and comfortable. They were made by digging into the rock.

▲ Castles usually had a strong tower called the keep. The outer wall was called the curtain wall. This is Rochester Castle which was built in England in the 1100's. Its walls are twelve feet thick.

## Keeping out the Enemy

In the past, people burned fires at night. Fires kept them warm, and also they kept wild animals away. People had to protect their own animals, too. They built a strong fence around their village. They left one small opening in it. At night, they herded the animals inside the fence. Then, guards could defend the way into the village. Some people in Africa still live in villages like this.

A hill made a safe place to live. Enemies could be seen easily if they tried to attack a village. Sometimes, the hill villages had a stone wall around them. These walled villages were called **hill forts**.

Enemies tried to take over the hill forts ıd villages. If they won the battle, they ould then live in the hill fort.

Strong, walled **castles** were built as ıfe places for rulers to live in. Families, ɪrvants, and soldiers all lived there. If ıere was danger, the people who lived earby could go into the castle for safety. hey brought their animals, too! In urope, between 1100 and 1500, whole ɔwns were often built within castle ɾalls. There were guards on the gates ıto the towns.

In some countries, people have to build houses ı very wet places. They may be close to marshy ivers or on land which floods easily. Stilts keep ıe homes above the water. These houses are on ıe Indonesian island of Sulawesi.

## Floods and Earthquakes

In some parts of the world, there is a danger of floods and earthquakes. Floods wash away buildings. People and animals are often drowned if they cannot get away in time. Earthquakes shake the ground. Buildings may fall down and kill people. Houses have to be built so that they remain safe.

Houses in Japan are in danger of earthquakes. They used to be built of paper and tall grass plants called **bamboo**. If they fell, they did not hurt people too much. Today, the Japanese build their houses on concrete blocks. The houses move as the ground moves. Building in this way means that fewer houses fall down in earthquakes.

# On the Move

Some people do not live in one place all the time. They travel around. They take their homes with them. In the past, people traveled around in search of food and often lived in tents. In some parts of the world, people still live in homes or mobile homes that they can move. Some live in tents or on boats. Others live in wagons. Today, mobile homes are often used by people on vacation.

## Tents

People who travel around are called **nomads**. Some North American peoples, such as the Sioux, Blackfoot, and Cheyenne, were nomads. In the 1500's, they hunted and farmed on the lands near the Rocky Mountains. Spanish explorers brought horses to North and South America. Horses made it easier for people to hunt for food. Many people gave up farming and became wandering hunters. They hunted bison mainly. They ate bison meat and they used th hides for many things. People's clothin and shoes were made of hides. The slept on fur rugs.

These nomadic people lived in con shaped tents called **tepees**. These we made from bison hides which we stretched over wooden poles. Becaus the hunters were often traveling, th tepees had to be light. When the wanted to move on, they folded th tepees and tied them to wooden frame These frames, called **travois**, wer dragged along by dogs or horses.

In many desert places, such as North Africa and the Middle East, nomadi people still travel with tents. Often, th tents are made from pressed animal hai called **felt**. They are carried by camels.

▼ The Bedouin are Arab people who live in the deserts of the Middle East. They travel across the desert to look for food for their flocks. They weave strips of cloth and sew them together. They use this cloth to make tents like these.

## iving on Boats

Goods were often carried from place to lace on rivers or on canals. It was easier ) move around on water than on land. he boats which carried the goods were alled **barges**. Families lived on these arges. In Europe, some of these old oats are now vacation homes. Others, uch as the barges on the Rhine River, re still permanent homes. Canal boats ısed to be pulled along by horses valking on the canal's banks. Today, hey are powered by engines.

▲ Hong Kong is a small island. It is very crowded. Many people live in boats around the island. Many of the boats, or sampans, in this picture are decorated for the Chinese New Year. The large, colorful boat is a floating restaurant.

## Wagons

In the 1800's, many people traveled across North America. They wanted to find new places to live. On the journey, their homes were wagons. The conastoga wagon was a cart with wooden hoops put up over the top. Cloth could be drawn over the hoops for shelter. These wagons were called "prairie schooners."

**Gypsies** are some of the last nomads in Europe. They used to travel in painted wagons that were pulled by horses. Today, some have trailers pulled by cars and some travel in vans. Many gypsies can no longer find places to camp. They are beginning to camp on sites that are kept just for them.

▲ The families who crossed North America used wagons like this. They took all their belongings with them. This made the wagons very heavy. They had to be drawn by large teams of horses or oxen.

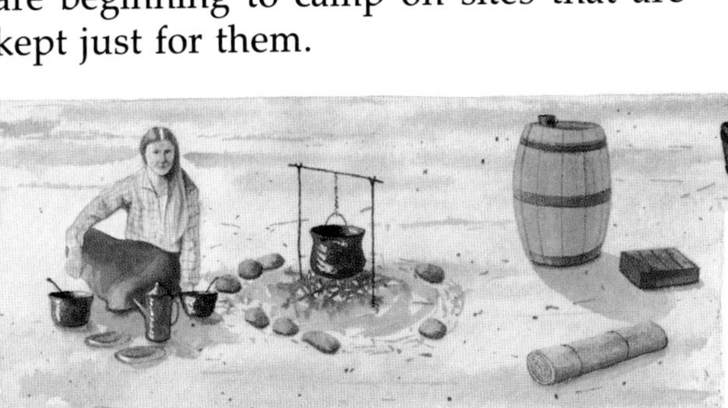

# Building Houses

People used to build their own homes. They built them out of whatever materials they could find. They decided the shape and the size of their homes. In some places, this still happens. Families build their own homes. They build them in the same way that people have always done. The way of building houses has not changed for thousands of years in these places.

In other places, styles of houses have changed. People used their homes differently. They wanted bigger rooms, or they wanted to decorate their houses. People began to pay workers to help them to build their homes, too.

▼ People make homes from the materials they find around them. These homes are made by the Dinka people in Sudan. They use grass held together by thin strips of wood from young trees.

## Builders

Bricklaying, tiling, and carpentry ar all skills, or **crafts**. They were used i Egypt and Babylon thousands of yea ago. The Romans developed new skil such as laying floors and carrying wate to homes.

Workers often learned a single craft. I Europe, about 500 years ago, craf workers formed groups called **guilds**. I order to join the guild, young worker had to prove that they were good at thei craft. Some of the crafts were wood o stonecarving, and glassmaking.

▼ Stonemasons carve stone. They have to use special stone that can be cut to the shape the builders need. Often, they carve decorations on it. Today, stonemasons still work like these stonemasons did in the 1500's.

▲ Andrea Palladio designed large villas, palaces, and churches. This villa is in the town of Vicenza in Italy. Palladio used tall columns and statues to make his buildings look like those built in Roman times.

In the past, it took many crafts people a long time to build a large house. Everything was done by hand. Today, using machines, building a house does not take as long. Windows, doors, sometimes even whole walls, are made in factories. They are brought to the building site ready-made. The builder fits them into place. Even a large house can be built quickly today.

## Planning Houses

Kings, queens, and other rulers wanted large, beautiful houses. They wanted to show other people how important they were. The builders of these houses needed drawings to help them. The drawings showed all the building details. These drawings are called **plans**.

People who draw plans for the builders are called **architects**. They want to make buildings strong and beautiful. They often learn from each other. Andrea Palladio was an Italian architect in the 1500's. He studied the work of the Roman architect named Vitruvius. Palladio wanted his buildings to look like Roman buildings. Many other architects learned from Palladio.

Today, many architects work as part of a building team. They work with new materials like steel and **plate glass**. They design apartment house complexes or housing developments.

# What Are Houses Made of?

People built houses out of whatever material they found nearby. In Papua New Guinea, it might be palm leaves and wood. In the deserts of the Middle East, it might be goatskin to make a tent. These materials last for awhile, but then they begin to rot.

Stone and brick last longer than grass or leaves. But stones and the bricks are heavy to carry. Today, many builders use new, lighter materials. They are easier to move around and they still make strong buildings.

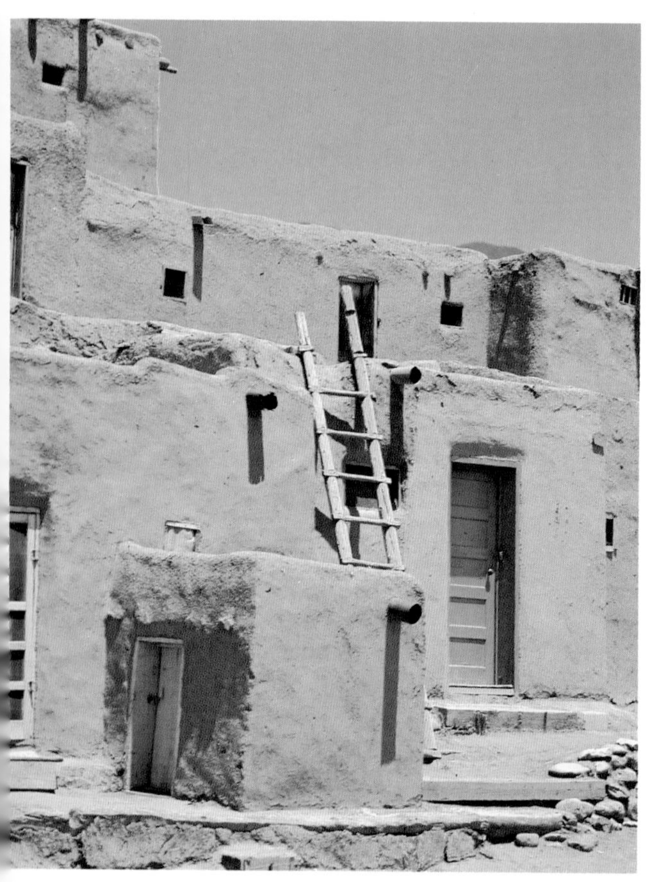

## Mud and Straw

Mud is easy to find and to use. Soil ca be mixed with water to form a paste. Th paste is left to dry in the sun and harde Houses were made in this way in ancie Egypt. In the Middle East, house several floors, or **stories**, high were bui from mud. In Europe, some earl cottages were built from layers of mu and straw.

## Leaves and Wood

Leaves and grasses are easy to carr and to press into shape, but they catc fire easily. Reeds were woven into mat and used as roofs, walls, and doors i places such as Peru in South America and in Southeast Asia. In Africa, gras was often used in the building of a home In forest areas, wood is a cheap building material. People who came to live in North America and Australia often made log cabins from whole tree trunks. The bark protected the wood from rotting. In other places, wooden frames and flat planks of wood were used. Planks need to be painted, polished, or varnished to protect them from the weather.

◀ The Pueblo Indians live in the southwest of the United States. Their traditional homes are made of a kind of clay called adobe. The windows are very small so that the sunlight cannot get in. This keeps their houses cool inside.

## ·icks

In hot, dry parts of the world, there are ·ten not many trees. There is no wood ·r building. Bricks made out of clay are ·ed. The clay dries very fast in the sun. colder countries, bricks have to be ·ked in ovens before they are hard ·ough to use. Then, they become ·rong and last a long time.

## tone

Stone is strong and lasts a long time. It cut, or **quarried**, out of solid rock. ·hen, the stone is shaped into blocks and ·rried to a building site. Different kinds ·f stone are often found in one country. ·ouses in each place were made from ·e stone that was nearby.

▲ This house in the Philippines is made from many different materials. Wood, bamboo, leaves, and rushes have been used. These grow nearby and are cheap. The builders have also used corrugated iron which has been made elsewhere.

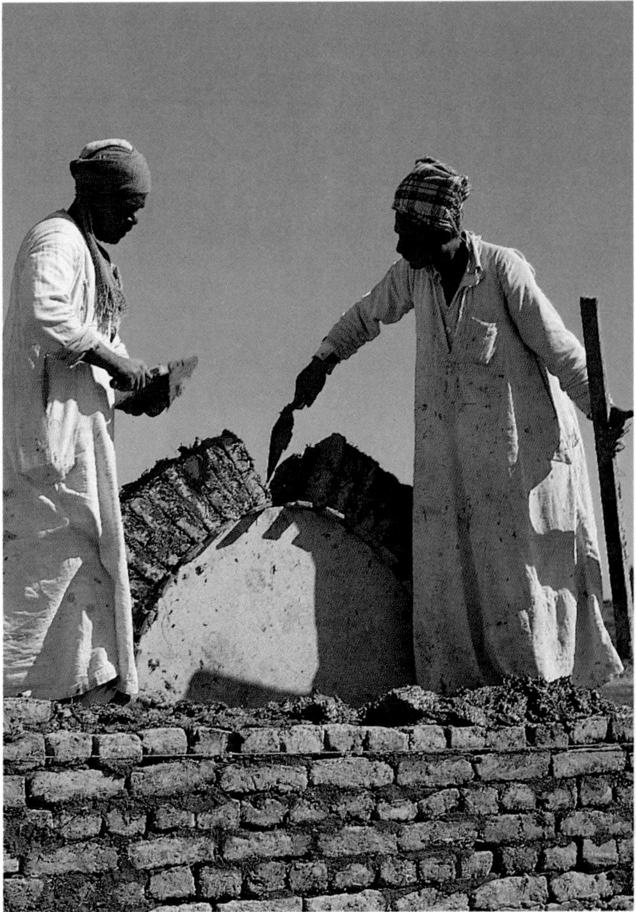

▲ These bricklayers are from Luxor in Egypt. Egyptians have made bricks like these for thousands of years. The bricks are held together with a mud mixture called mortar.

## Concrete and Cement

Almost 2,000 years ago, the architect Vitruvius described a rock powder which could be mixed with a white, powdered rock, called lime, and stones. This mixture was so hard that it would set even under water. Vitruvius named this rock powder "cementum." We call it cement. Concrete is made from a mixture of small stones, sand, water, and cement powder. The mixture hardens very fast.

# Roofs and Walls

Every house needs a roof. The shape of the roof depends on the climate. It also depends on the materials from which it is made.

## Protection from the Weather

In hot, dry countries, houses often have flat roofs. These keep the rooms below cool. Sometimes, stairs lead up to the roof. In the evenings, when the sun has gone down, people like to sit or sleep there. Some roofs have a very slight slope. If there is any rain, the water will drain away down the slope.

▼ The roofs of these Swiss houses are very steep. The snow is like a blanket on top of the roof. When the snow begins to melt, it runs off the roof easily. The roof hangs out over the walls to keep the snow from blocking the windows and doors.

In wet countries, houses have ste roofs. The rain runs down the slope the roof and is kept off the wal Sometimes, it drains into water channe called **gutters**. These gutters collect t water from the roof. A drainpipe carri the water from the gutters to the groun

## Roofing Materials

In countries such as Nepal and t United States, houses near forest are use wooden tiles called **shingles** for the roofs. In other places, roofs are made clay tiles or with blue-grey **slates**. Slate a rock that splits easily into thin, fl pieces.

In some countries, houses have roo made of straw, reeds, turf, or gras These are called **thatched** roofs. They ar warm in the winter and cool in th summer, but they catch fire easily. Afte awhile, they rot and have to be replaced

▲ Thatched roofs are found in many parts of the world. This house is in South Korea. Thatch is easy to make and it is cheap. The straw, grass, or reeds that are used can be found nearby.

Today, factory-made roofing materials are often used. These last a long time and make roofs watertight.

## Walls

The walls of a house have to be strong. They hold up the roof and any upper floors. Sometimes, walls are decorated. There may be stone carvings or patterns made out of brick, wood, or stone. Sometimes, the walls are painted with bright colors.

▼ In Mauritania in West Africa, the houses are made from clay. They are decorated with a traditional design. There are clay homes in other parts of Africa, too. These are also decorated, sometimes with bright colors.

In Europe about 500 years ago, people began to hang cloths on their inside walls. These wall hangings were called **tapestries**. They were pictures woven with brightly-colored thread. The tapestries helped to keep the house warm. Later, carpets brought back by traders from Asia were also hung on the walls. Sometimes, inner walls were covered with carved panels of wood.

Wallpaper was first used in Asia. In the 1600's, people in Europe began to copy the designs used on Chinese wallpapers. The wallpapers were painted by hand. They were very expensive. They were not pasted to the wall, but were framed in long, wooden panels. Wallpaper has become cheaper in the last hundred years. It can now be printed in rolls by machines.

# Doors and Windows

The first houses had no doors. The entrance to the house was sometimes covered with hides or branches. When wooden doors were made, they were attached to the doorposts. A small flap of wood or metal, called a **hinge**, allowed the door to move. The door could be opened to let in light and air. It could be closed for warmth and safety.

Houses were often shared with animals. Often, doors were made so that the top and bottom worked separately. They could be opened at the top to let in the light. The bottom half could be kept closed to keep animals in or out.

Sometimes, doors, or gates, had to be very large so that carts and horses could go through them. The big gates were too heavy to open all the time. Often, they had small doors cut into them. These little doors were called **wicket** gates.

The doors of palaces, castles an mansions were often very beautifu Often, wooden doors were carved wit flowers or leaves. Sometimes, doo were made of a metal called **bronze**. Th bronze was shaped with special tools t create scenes and decorations.

On some houses, doors are covered b roofs held up by pillars. These are calle **porches**. Porches are very useful. Peopl waiting in the rain or the hot sun can tak shelter under porches.

▼ Doors can be plain or decorated. Some doors are very large. They are used in castles or farms. Revolving doors were used where many people would go in and out.

decorated doorway of the 1800's

wicket gate

stable door

revolving door

# /indows

The first windows were just narrow its in a wall. They let in a little light, but ey kept the rain out. Very few indows had glass in them because glass as very expensive. Wooden shutters or ieces of animal horn were used instead. lany houses had wooden shutters. /indow glass used to be made from lown glass. The bubble of glass was fted away from the blowpipe by an iron ube. The tube left a blob in the glass. 'ou can see these whirls in the middle of ld glass window panes.

In the late 1700's, a new style of vindow was invented in England. These vere opened and closed by sliding them ıp or down. They were called **sash** vindows. They could be opened at the op or the bottom.

Glassmakers found out how to make oigger sheets of glass. Window panes oecame larger. Today, steel frames can nold up the roof or the upper stories of a house. As a result, whole walls can be made of sheets of plate glass.

▼ This house is in Rajasthan in India. Some of the windows have shutters. These block out the light. They block out the heat as well. The other windows are covered by a carved screen. This lets in air and some light through the fine holes.

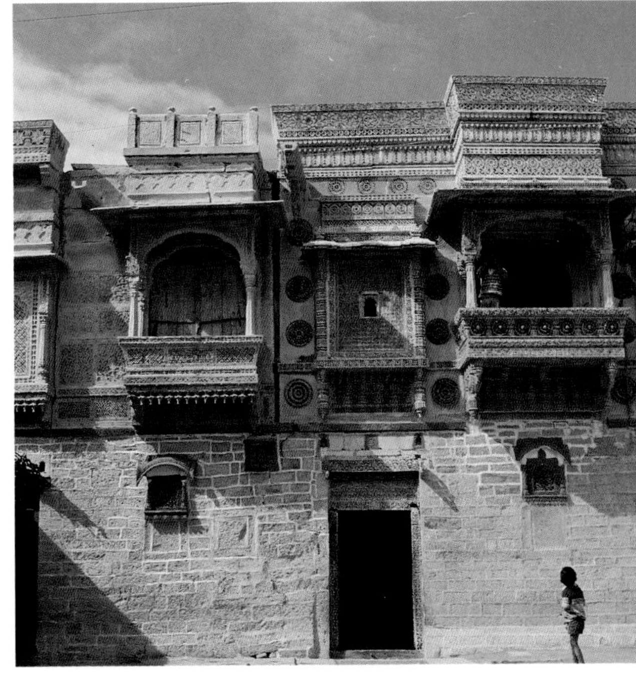

▼ The first windows had no glass. This was a problem because they let cold air in as well as light. Even when glass was invented, it was very expensive. Glass was not made in large sheets, but in small panes.

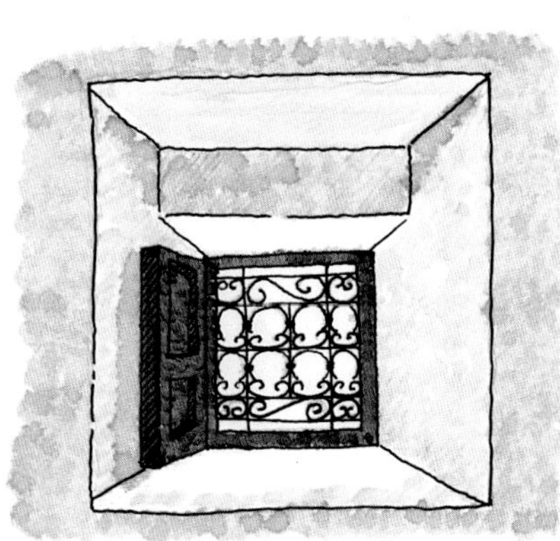

North African window

early European window

sash window

# Keeping Houses Safe

The first doors were closed with wooden bars called **latches**. The latch was fastened to the door. It was held by another piece of wood on the doorpost. People lifted the latch to open the door. Latches made it possible to keep out the wind and animals. They were easy to open from the outside, so they did not keep out thieves.

Another simple way to close a door is to use a **bolt**. A bolt is a sliding piece of wood or metal attached to the door. It pushes into a hollow in the doorpost. An inside bolt can act as a lock. Doors cannot be locked from the outside with a bolt.

▲ A latch is the most simple way of keeping a door closed. They are used on doors that do not need to be locked. A bolt helps keep people out. It can only work on one side of a door. A padlock can lock the bolt so it cannot be moved.

▲ These are locksmiths in the 1600's. They did all their work by hand. The keys and locks they made were very large and heavy. The keys were also quite easy to copy.

## Locks

The earliest way of locking a door from the outside was used in Egypt about 4,000 years ago. A wooden bolt was made with three holes in it. When it was pushed into the lock, three pegs fell into the holes. The key to the lock had three pegs in it, too. When it was pushed under the bolt, it raised the three pegs out of the holes.

About 2,000 years ago, the Romans made metal locks. These locks used a different kind of key. Ridges on the key pushed a spring, which made a bolt fall into place. These **spring locks** were the first to have small keys that were easy to carry.

Four hundred years ago, large iron cks were first made in Europe. The ys were easy to copy, so the locks were ot very safe. In 1818, Jeremiah Chubb vented a new kind of lock. Each key ad six or more small cuts, or **notches**, at e end. These were cut at different vels on each key. The key had to match e lock exactly to open it. The Chubb ck made houses much safer from ieves.

In 1861, Linus Yale invented an even afer lock. The key has notches all along s edge. When it is pushed into a tube, it ushes up metal pins. The pins fit the ey notches.This means the key can turn he tube to unlock the catch on the door.

Some locks have a dial. There are numbers on the dial. You have to move the dial around to the numbers in the right order. If you get the order wrong, the lock will not open. These **combination locks** are not new. Pictures of this same kind of lock have been found that are dated 1420. These locks are only used in houses if people want to keep something especially safe. People who have very valuable things or a lot of money in their homes use combination locks.

Today, many people also keep their homes safe with burglar alarms and hidden cameras. These warn the owner or the police if someone tries to break in.

Yale lock

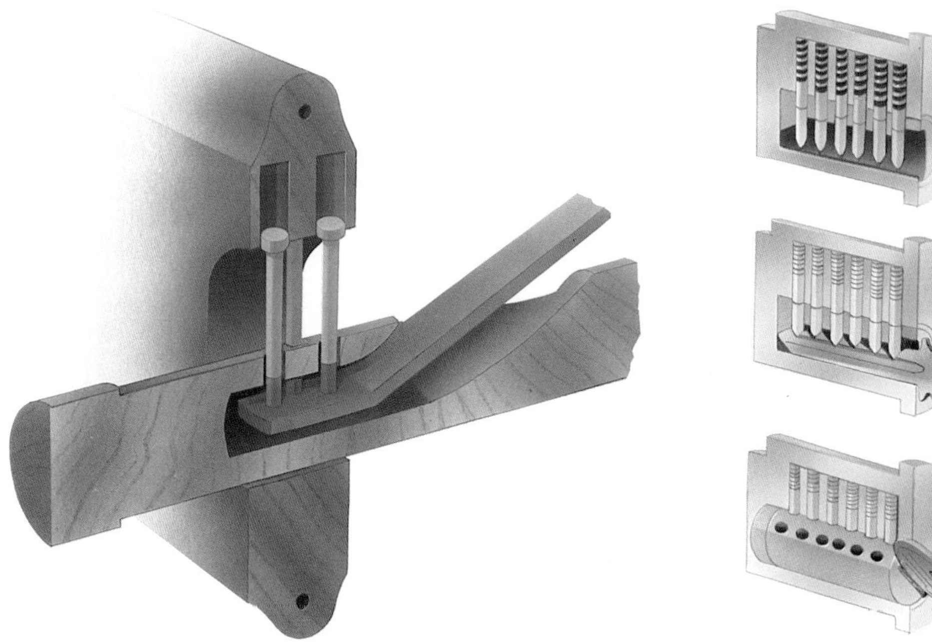

Egyptian locking bolt

People tried several kinds of locks. They needed something strong and secure. They also needed something small and light. No one wanted to carry huge, heavy keys around with them.

# Floors and Ceilings

The earliest floors were made of earth. Sometimes, they were covered with **rushes** to keep them warm and dry. The rushes were replaced when they became dirty. Stone, brick, and tile floors have also been used for hundreds of years. They are very useful in kitchens where the floor needs to be washed often.

In hot countries, people used marble for floors because it stays cool. The Romans made patterned floors. They made pictures with colored chips of marble. The chips were set in cement. These patterns are called **mosaics**.

In colder countries, floors were ofte covered with hides or rugs made out c rags. Carpets were very expensive. In th 1800's, a cheap floor covering was mad with canvas and linseed oil. This wa called **linoleum**, and it became ver popular.

## Carpets

Nomad peoples in the Middle East us carpets as furniture. They sit on then and sleep on them. When they move on they roll up their carpets and carry then along with their tents.

◀ The Romans made patterned mosaic floor for their villas. In the main rooms, they had pictures like the one in the center of this floor. It took a long time to lay a mosaic floor. Clay tiles were quicker and cheaper to use. They are still popular in hot parts of the world.

From the 1200's to the 1500's, the first ırpets came by boat to Europe from hina, India, and Turkey. They had ɪight and colorful patterns. Only very ·ealthy people could afford them. At rst, they were draped over chests and ıbles. They were too precious to walk n. They were also hung on the walls like aintings, or used to cover beds.

By the 1700's, carpets were being made ı Europe. Many towns such as Wilton, ı England, have given their names to ypes of carpets. Carpet-making in actories began in the United States in the ate 1700's. Making carpets in factories neant that they were much cheaper. More people could buy them.

▲ This boy is in Pakistan. He is weaving a traditional carpet. The first carpets brought to Europe were made in the same way. It takes a very long time to make a carpet by hand. There are many different patterns made from dyed wool or cotton.

▲ This ceiling was designed in the 1700's by a man named Robert Adam. The patterns are of flowers, fruit, and leaves. They are molded from plaster and then attached to the ceiling.

## Ceilings

Early ceilings were also the floor of the room above. You could see all the wooden beams, or supports, which held up the boards. Sometimes, the beams were carved or painted. In the 1500's and 1600's, the ceilings of important rooms in large European houses were covered. A mixture of lime, sand, and water was used. This mixture was called **plaster**. Often, there were shapes and patterns in the plaster. Some ceilings were made of smooth plaster. They were painted with pictures. Today, most ceilings are plastered. The beams of the floor above cannot be seen.

# Stairs and Elevators

In the first houses, everyone lived, ate, and slept on the ground floor. There were no upper floors. The houses were often crowded. When people wanted more room, they built a platform above the ground. They used a ladder to climb up to it. The platform was a place to store things. Hay or bedding could be kept there.

When people found out how to buil upper floors, they needed a safe way t reach them. They learned how to buil stairs. Then, they could build muc bigger houses. The houses could b several stories high.

## Stairs

Staircases take up a lot of space. Th first staircases were often built outsid houses. Sometimes, in bigger houses the stairs were built inside a rounc tower. The stairs went around a centra pillar. Stairs like this are called **spira** staircases. They were made from wood stone, or brick. Often, they were very steep and there was not much light.

In the 1500's, carpenters built sloping wooden staircases. They carved faces, flowers, and plants on the bannisters and on the posts. In the 1700's, large staircases were built out of marble. They were very grand. They were often the central feature of the house.

Today, most staircases are not as grand. They are not too steep, and they are often covered with carpet.

◀ This painting is from a medieval manuscript showing the Tower of Babel being built. The artist painted it in the style of his own time. He has shown the Tower of Babel being built like a tower from the Middle Ages. It has an outside staircase.

▲ There are carved wooden staircases like this one in many old houses in Europe. This staircase was built in 1701. It is in Hanbury Hall near Worcester, in England.

## Elevators

People have known how to make buildings several stories high for a very long time. Old buildings of four or five stories are found in many parts of the world. People who lived in tall buildings had many stairs to climb. They must have been very tired when they reached the top floor.

In 1852, Elisha Graves Otis invented a safe elevator. This kind of elevator could carry people to the top of any building.

After elevators were invented, even higher buildings could be built. In places like New York City, the buildings are so tall that they are called "skyscrapers." Some of them are over one hundred stories high. In some new skyscrapers, elevators with glass walls travel up and down on the outside of the buildings. The people using these elevators can enjoy the view outside.

▼ This elevator was raised by a pole pushing from underneath. The elevator could only go up a few stories. When the pulley elevator was invented, elevators could travel up many floors.

# Heating the Home

We do not know how people first learned to make fire. Perhaps, they saw lightning strike a tree, or perhaps the sun set dry grass on fire. Fire gives heat and light. But it is also dangerous. It can destroy our homes and woodlands.

Wood fires heated homes for thousands of years. People cooked on fires. They also used fire to keep wild animals away. In the 1200's, Marco Polo, an Italian explorer, saw coal being burned in China. In Europe, wood and pressed earth, called **peat**, were burned. After the 1600's, more coal was burned by people in Europe.

## Chimneys

The first houses had no chimneys. Th
fire was built in the middle of the floo
From there, the smoke found its way ou
of a hole in the roof. Often, the room
would be filled with smoke. The peopl
and objects in the room would becom
filthy with smoke dust. This smoke dus
is called soot.

When people built fireplaces, th
smoke went up through a small chimne
called a **flue**. The flue was added on t
the outside of the house. The first flue
were wooden and were lined with clay
Sometimes, they caught fire. By th
1400's, chimneys were being built o
brick or stone. They did not catch fire a
easily as the wood and clay chimneys.

The soot made by coal smoke can block chimneys. In the 1800's, small boys worked as chimney sweeps. They crawled into the open fireplaces and up into the chimneys. Then, they brushed the soot down to the fireplace.

▼ At first, there were no chimneys. People lit firs on the floor. Later, they built the fire near a wall. They put high walls around the fires. The smoke went up between these walls. These were the beginnings of chimneys. Houses were very dark inside. People got up at sunrise and went to bed at sunset.

Often, large houses had very large chimneys. veral fireplaces opened out into one chimney. ese chimneys became very sooty. Young boys mbed up the chimneys to clean them. It was a ngerous and very dirty job.

## Central Heating

The Romans invented the first kind of central heating. They built a closed fire, or **furnace**, below their houses. The hot air rose through the floors and behind the walls to an opening in the roof. But during the Middle Ages, this idea was lost. Central heating was not used again for more than a thousand years.

The United States was one of the first countries where central heating was used again. In 1877, a group of houses was heated from one central place. Pipes took the heat to the houses. In some parts of Russia, Denmark, and Germany, this type of heating is used today.

Central heating came to Europe in the late 1800's. People found new ways of heating water and air. These systems can be run by oil, electricity, or gas. The heat travels along pipes or through vents. We can choose when to turn the heat on or off. We can also choose how hot to make our homes. We can also set a timer to turn the heat on and off.

There is a new kind of heating which uses the sun's rays. It is called **solar heating**. Panels covered with glass are put on the roof to attract the sun's rays. This heats the water that is running through the panels to a boiler. The boiler provides hot water and central heating for the house.

▲This house is in the state of New Mexico. It has been designed to use the sun's rays. The roof catches heat from the sun. This is used to heat water. The hot water heats the house.

# Lighting the Home

Before glass was used, windows were just small openings in the walls. Houses were very dark inside. People got up at sunrise and went to bed at sunset.

## Lamps and Candles

The first lamps were made from clay or stone. Vegetable oils or the fat of some animals were burned. These lamps did not smell very nice. Candles made from beeswax smelled sweeter than oil lamps. Most people could not afford these candles. They made their own candles. They dipped rushes in fat and burned them. The rushes were a kind of **wick**. They kept the flame burning. Candles were used by most people until the mid-1800's. There was no other way to light a home or workplace.

▼ Lighting used to come from small oil lamps or candles. But these lights were not very bright. The first good lighting came from paraffin lamps, invented in the 1800's. Later, lighting by gas was invented. The best light of all is made by electricity.

In Europe, in the 1700's, some of the bigger houses had beautiful hanging lamps. These lamps had a large metal frame with candle holders all around it. The big lamps held hundreds of candles. They were called **chandeliers**. Often, pieces of glass were hung all over the lamps. The candlelight made the glass sparkle. Chandeliers could be lowered from the ceiling on chains, so that people could light and put out the candles.

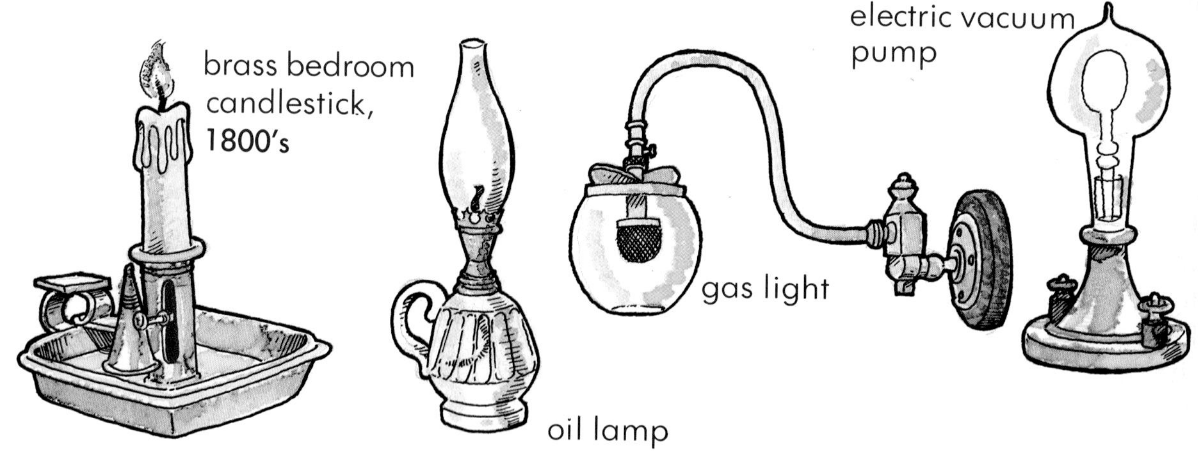

◀ Chandeliers are usually hung with pieces of glass. The glass is cut at different angles. The candlelight is reflected by the glass. This makes the candlelight much brighter. Chandeliers must be kept clean to work well. They are difficult to clean and to light.

## Gaslights and Paraffin Lamps

By the 1840's, some houses in the United States and Europe had gas lighting. It was not very bright. The lights flickered and were sooty. In 1859, oil was found in Pennsylvania. **Paraffin** was produced from oil. It was not expensive and gave a bright light. These paraffin lamps were not very safe. Paraffin is a liquid and it catches fire easily. If a lamp were knocked over, the whole house could be burned down.

## The Electric Light Bulb

In 1748, an important discovery was made. The American scientist, Benjamin Franklin, flew a kite in a storm. He saw that the metal key on the kite attracted lightning. When the lightning struck the key, there was a spark. Franklin knew that electricity caused this. The key let electricity pass through it. But one knew how to store and use this energy.

In the late 1870's, two men were working on ideas for electric lamps. In 1878, Joseph Swan made the first electric light bulb. In October, 1879, Thomas Alva Edison made a light bulb which glowed for forty hours. Joseph Swan worked with an electrical current and metal rods. He put a thin rod into a glass bulb. The rod was made of **carbon**. Then, he took all the air out of the bulb. When he passed an electric current through the rod, it glowed brightly inside the bulb. By the late 1880's, light bulbs were being made in the United States.

In the 1900's, homes began to be lighted by electric light. At first, some people were afraid of electricity. They thought it could leak out from the light switch.

▼ Joseph Swan and Thomas Edison worked together to produce light bulbs.

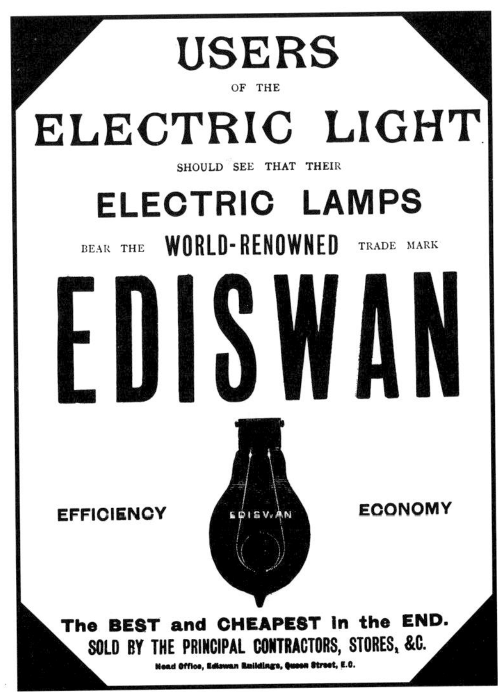

USERS
OF THE
ELECTRIC LIGHT
SHOULD SEE THAT THEIR
ELECTRIC LAMPS
BEAR THE WORLD-RENOWNED TRADE MARK
EDISWAN
EFFICIENCY
EDISWAN
ECONOMY
The BEST and CHEAPEST in the END.
SOLD BY THE PRINCIPAL CONTRACTORS, STORES, &C.
Head Office, Ediswan Buildings, Queen Street, E.C.

# The Water Supply

If we had no water, we would soon die. Crops cannot grow without water. In places where there is no rain, people starve. In many parts of the world, clean water comes out of a faucet. Dirty water goes down a drain. Yet, in other parts of the world, water has to be carried long distances. It comes from rivers, lakes, and wells. When it rains, the water is collected and stored carefully.

## Wells and Pumps

A well is a store of water below the ground. One old Chinese well was said to be nearly 1,625 feet deep. Villages and towns grew up beside rivers or lakes, or near springs and wells. At first, the water was pulled up from the wells in buckets. Then, pumps were made. The water was pumped up by hand or by machine. It was carried back to the home in buckets or in water jugs. This was hard work. People soon tried to find a better way to bring water into their homes.

## Storing Water

About 3,000 years ago, in the cities of Jordan in the Middle East, people built water tunnels. These were called **conduits**. They carried water from rivers and lakes into the city. Each house had its own tank for water. This water tank was called a **cistern**. The cistern stored the water that flowed in from the conduits.

▼ This water cistern is in the remains of the ancient city of Carthage in North Africa. This cistern was built by the Romans to store water which came from mountains many miles away.

## ’ater Channels

Water cannot flow uphill, so water .nnels did not work in hilly country. .ne Romans solved this problem 2,000 ›ars ago. They built special bridges .lled **aqueducts**. These carried the water .igh across the valleys.

The Romans ruled many parts of .urope. Wherever they lived, they built ’ater pipes and pumps. These brought ,vater to public fountains and baths. Vhen the Roman Empire came to an end ,500 years ago, the water systems were ›ft to fall into ruins.

▼ The Romans made sure their cities had good ,vater supplies. This aqueduct is in France, but it vas built by the Romans. The water ran along a .hannel on the top.

## Today’s Water

Today, many people have hot and cold water tanks in their homes. Other people still collect water from a river or well. The weather can cause many problems. In very hot countries, the rivers and wells will sometimes dry up during the dry season. In cold countries, the water freezes. Even the water in pipes can freeze, too. Since we all need water to stay alive, these problems have to be solved.

▼ There are still many people in the world who do not have water in their homes. They have to get water from a public faucet, a well, or a river. This woman in India is carrying water home in the pots on her head.

# Pipes and Drains

Some people in the past knew that houses had to have a supply of clean water. They also knew how to get rid of dirty water and waste matter. Five thousand years ago, in the Indus valley of Pakistan, there were brick houses with drains. These drains carried away the dirty water. In Rome, the lavatories were joined to pipes under the ground called sewers. The sewers were kept flushed by running water. This carried waste, or **sewage**, outside the city. Later, all this knowledge was forgotten.

▲ This sketch was from a newspaper of the 1850's. It was drawn to show the terrible slums of London. Houses were crowded and dirty. There was no clean water or drainage. There were many diseases. Doctors and other people fought for good drainage and clean water.

▲ The channels in the ground are drains. They were built 5,000 years ago in the city of Mohenjo-Daro in Pakistan. The city had a regular drainage system. Closed pipes came from the houses to these open channels. The channels were cleaned to keep them clear.

Four hundred years ago, in most cities in Europe, houses did not have clean water. Water was brought from rivers and lakes to the street pumps. This water was often dirty since the pipes were open to the air. Water carriers sold fresh spring water in the streets. Spring water was cleaner, but there were no lids on the buckets, so dirt got into the water. There were no drains under the ground. There were only gutters to carry dirty water away. Gutters were at the side of, or down the middle of, the streets. Dirty water and waste were often thrown out from windows into the street below. Many towns in the world still have drains above ground like this.

## irty Water and Disease

Many people left the countryside to ıd work in the cities. The cities became ery crowded. Lavatories often emptied to holes, called **cesspools**, under the ouses. The water in wells and rivers as made dirty by sewage leaking from ıe cesspools. People died of diseases ıch as **cholera** and **typhoid fever**. They id not know that they caught these iseases from dirty water.

By the 1800's, some doctors found out ıat very small living creatures called **erms** cause disease. The cholera and yphoid germs lived in dirty water. The vater had been infected by waste matter. People had been using the dirty water for drinking or cooking. In this way, killer diseases spread. More and more people died. It was clear that something had to be done.

## Sewage Systems

In the 1800's, systems of underground sewers were built in Europe and the United States. Roads were dug up and underground tunnels were built. Drain pipes were then connected to the houses. People said the costs were too high, but fewer people died from diseases. Today, many cities all over the world have underground sewers. There are still many places where there are no proper drainpipes to carry sewage away.

In the 1870s, large underground sewers were ›uilt to carry away the waste and dirty water. They are still used today.

# Kitchens

A place for cooking food has always been important. Sometimes, the kitchen was in a separate building. This was usually for safety in case of fire. In small houses, the kitchen was often the only warm room. It was used for living, eating, and sleeping.

Most of the cooking was done in the fireplace. A large pot, or **cauldron**, was used to boil food. It hung over the fire on metal chains. Soup, stew, or gruel was cooked in it. Meat was roasted over the fire. A metal pole, called a **spit**, was stuck through the meat. The spit rested on a frame just above the flames. It could be turned, so that the meat cooked all around. Brick ovens were built in the walls or chimney near the fire. These were used for baking.

## Cooking Stoves

In the 1700's and 1800's, many kitchen fires were of coal instead of wood. Metal fireplaces, called **ranges**, were built. These had iron ovens and plates to put pots and pans on. Ranges were polished with a paste called **black lead**.

The first gas ovens were used in the 1870's. These new ovens did not work very well. Sometimes, there was not enough gas and the flame went out. Today, gas, electric, and microwave ovens are used. They are easy to use and easy to clean.

▲ This is a kitchen in France in the 1800's. It has a large range. Part of the range held hot water. The water came out of the faucets at the side. O the walls, are all the pots and tools used for cooking.

▲ The first ovens were used mainly for baking bread. Many people had no ovens. They took their pies and cakes to the baker. He would put them in his oven after he had baked the bread.

## toring Food

Food that is kept too long will go bad. n the past, it was difficult to keep food or long. People tried to keep their food ool. Sometimes, meat was kept in a et-covered frame. This was called a **neat safe**. The safe let air cool the food, ut kept the flies away. Cupboards, alled **larders**, were often built in the oolest part of the house. There were air holes in the wall. They let in fresh air. People also stored food in cellars.

The first machine which cooled air was invented in the United States in 1834. With this machine, food could be kept fresh for days. The machine was called a **refrigerator**. It was invented by Jacob Perkins. In the 1920's, another American, Clarence Birdseye, found a way to freeze food. Today, many kitchens have freezers. Food can be stored in them for months.

▶ The first washing machines looked like this. The washing was done in the tub. The handle moved the water and clothes around. The mangle was used to wring out the clothes.

## Washing Clothes

Washing is not always done in the kitchen. Sometimes, washing is done outside in rivers or lakes. In some houses, a special room is used for washing. It is best to have hot water. During the 1800's, water was heated in a tub on the fire or range. The clothes were washed by thumping a wooden **dolly** up and down in the hot water. A dolly looked like a three-legged stool with a long pole stuck through its center. The water was squeezed out of the clothes by the rollers of a **mangle**. In 1907, an American named Alva J. Fisher, made a washing machine. It had an electric motor. The motor moved a dolly up and down in the water.

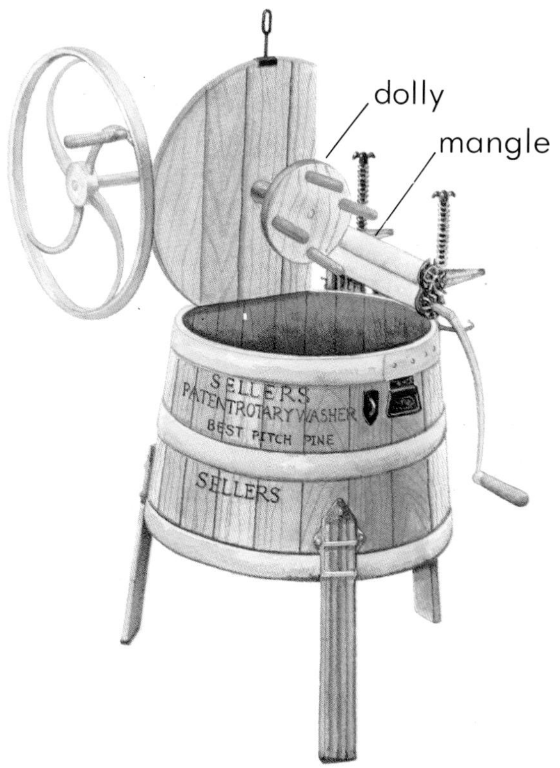

# Dining Rooms

In Europe, about 1,000 years ago, groups of people often ate their meals together in a room called a great hall. Tables were used only for meals. When the meal was finished, the wooden table top was lifted off its legs, or **trestle**. It was then propped up against the wall.

In their own homes, most people ate in the room where they lived. Then, wealthy families began to use one room just for eating. These dining rooms were for special occasions.

## Table Manners

Between the 1100's and the 1500's, if you were about nine or ten, you would have started your first job. You might have been sent to live with another family. There, you would be a maid or a page. You would have to learn good table manners. You could not throw meat or fishbones under the table. You ate with your fingers. Everybody had a large piece of bread to eat with their meals. They broke off lumps of the bread to dip into the sauce or gravy. Also, the bread was used to scoop food out of the bowl. Knives were used only for cutting very tough food. Forks were not used until the 1500's.

▲ These people are Japanese. They are eating in a traditional way. They are kneeling at a very low table. The food is served in small bowls. People eat with chopsticks. Some of the food is eaten raw, like sushi.

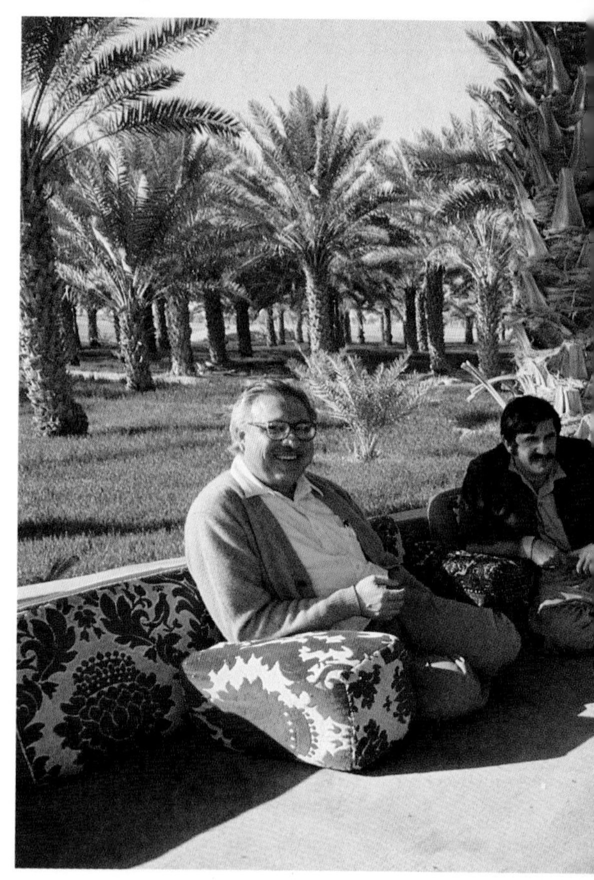

▶ People all over the world enjoy eating outside. These men and boys are in Saudi Arabia. They are sitting on a carpet, and eating spicy food from one large bowl. Their religion says that they must eat with their right hands only.

## alt

Salt was very precious. In the days ·fore refrigerators, covering meat with ılt was the only way to keep it from ɔing bad. A large pot, or **saltcellar**, ood in the middle of every table. If the ımily was wealthy, the saltcellar was ıade of silver or gold. Important people ıt near the head of the table. This was above" the saltcellar. The other people ıt at the bottom end of the table below ıe saltcellar. This is where the xpression "below the salt" comes from.

• In houses where important people lived, there vas usually a dining hall with a large table. This arved oak table is long, so that many people an sit at it. People often sat on benches.

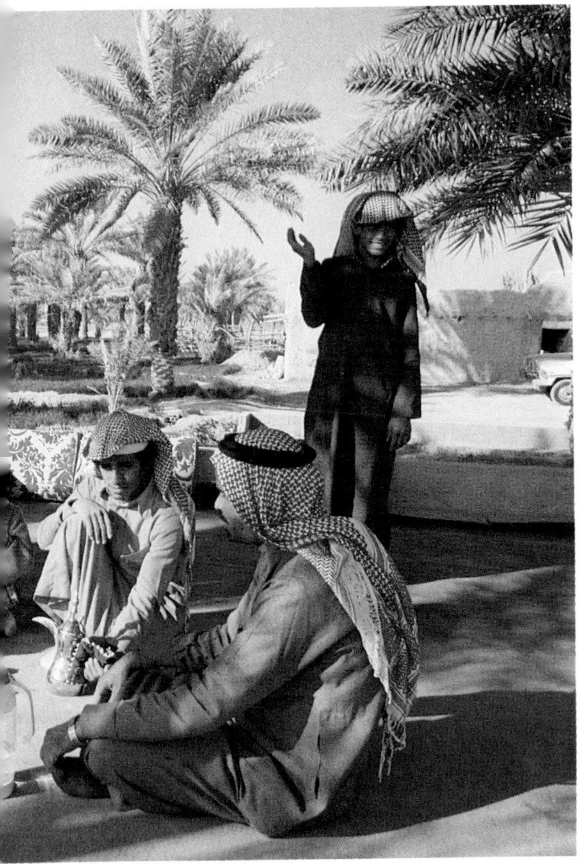

## Tables and Chairs

Kitchen furniture was plain and simple. It was made by local carpenters. They used strong wood such as oak, elm, or yew. Dining room furniture was for guests to see and admire. The wood was often carved and polished. In the 1500's, in Europe, it was made from oak. By the 1800's, South American woods were also used. People liked light furniture. It could be finely carved. Tables and chairs were made from woods such as walnut, maple, or rosewood.

## The Dumbwaiter

In the 1800's, the kitchen was often in the basement of large homes. It took a long time to carry food from the kitchen to the dining room. The food would get cold. Sometimes, houses had a small hand-operated elevator. This was called a dumbwaiter. The food was pulled up to the dining room on the dumbwaiter.

# Living Rooms

Until about 200 years ago, people lived and worked in one room. This was used for cooking and might have to be shared with animals. Very few families had separate rooms where they could sit to relax in comfort. In hot countries, like Greece and India, there was often a shady inner courtyard. People could sit there in the evenings.

▼ Some homes in China are often small. They only have a few rooms. The family cooks, eats and sits in the living room. They keep many of their belongings there, too.

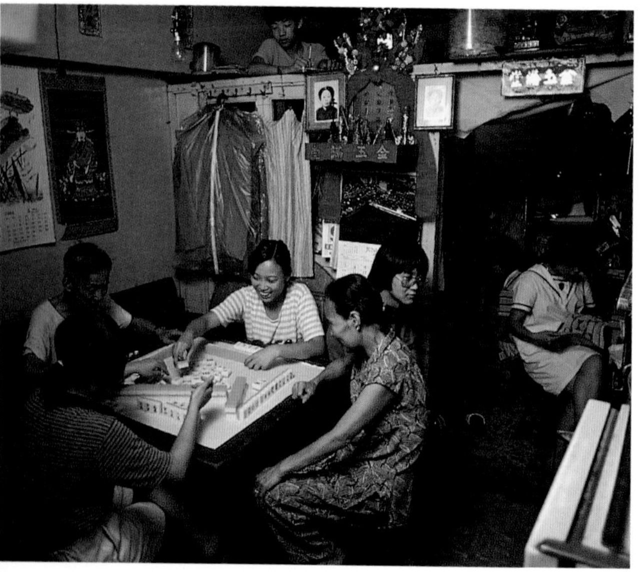

## Cushions and Seats

The first seating was very simple. People sat on animal furs, or brushwood, or just on stones or logs. In Asia, carpets and cushions were used to sit on. In many old paintings, you can see Indian rulers sitting on heaps of silk cushions. Other people had to sit on the floor.

In Europe, chairs were first made of wood or stone. They were draped with rugs or furs. Living rooms in most houses were furnished only with tables and hard chairs.

Toward the end of the 1700's, chairs and sofas were made with padded seats and arms. This was called **upholstery**. All the work was done by hand. In the late 1800's, wooden furniture was beginning to be made in factories. The furniture was less expensive, so more people could afford to buy it.

## The First Sitting Rooms

Wealthy people had houses with many rooms. Large Greek and Roman houses had separate rooms where the family and their friends could sit and talk. They were often built to face south, so that they would be sunny in wintertime.

In Europe, some of the first living rooms were upstairs. They were built to catch the sunshine. These rooms were called **solars**. They were used by the family. Sometimes, a second room was built upstairs, where the women could sit and talk while sewing. This was called the **parlor**.

Town houses were built with upper stories. The top floor was often made into a long **gallery**. Here, people could walk on rainy days. They could entertain their friends.

## Drawing Rooms

After 1700, people in many countries had furnished rooms where they sat after dinner. They drank tea and talked with friends. These were called **withdrawing rooms**. Later, they were just called drawing rooms. In the largest and grandest houses, they were sometimes called **salons**.

By the end of the 1800's, more families could afford to have a house with a living room. This was often a showplace for friends to admire. It was only used on Sundays and for special occasions.

▲ The long gallery was often used during bad weather. The children played and had lessons there. People talked and read by the fireplace, or walked for exercise. Music and dancing also took place in the gallery.

▼ This is a drawing room in the 1870's. It belonged to the Hatch family. The curtains are heavy and shut out the sunlight. The room is crowded with dark furniture.

# Bedrooms

For thousands of years, most people slept on the floor. Others slept on platforms around the edges of a room. People did not have separate rooms for sleeping.

In some hot countries, people have always slept in **hammocks**. These are made from cloth or woven leaves. Hammocks can be tied up between two trees or two posts. They are light and easy to carry around.

## Beds

Thousands of years ago, the Egyptians had beds that were the same shape as the beds of today. The Greeks and Romans had couches. They used "daybeds" for lying on at a feast or banquet.

For a long time, only very wealth people had beds. But they had no speci bedroom. Beds were kept on a raise platform at one end of the hall. The were curtains around the bed calle hangings. These hangings kept out th drafts of cold air.

In some parts of Europe, countr people slept on straw or on mattresse filled with leaves or feathers. Beds i cottages were very simple. They wer like cupboards in the wall. They ha doors that closed over them in th daytime.

By the 1500's, the **four-poster bed** wa popular. It had curtains all around it. A four-poster bed gave privacy ever though other people shared the room Often, children and servants slept in the same room as the house owner. Thei beds were like drawers on wheels. They could be tucked under the big bed during the day. These beds were called **trundle beds**.

Eyptian bed, 2690 BC

▲ Beds have not changed much over the years. Beds in ancient Egypt looked like beds today. Some beds in the past were very large. Several people could sleep in them.

large bed from an inn

◀ A futon is used as a bed in Japan. It is a thick cotton mattress laid on the floor. The pillow is supported by a separate woven frame and the bed is covered by a warm quilt. Japanese homes are not usually large. People fold futon beds away during the day to save space.

▼ This Chinese bed has a hard base covered with a woven rush mat. The bed has curtains which cover it completely. They are drawn together at night to keep out insects.

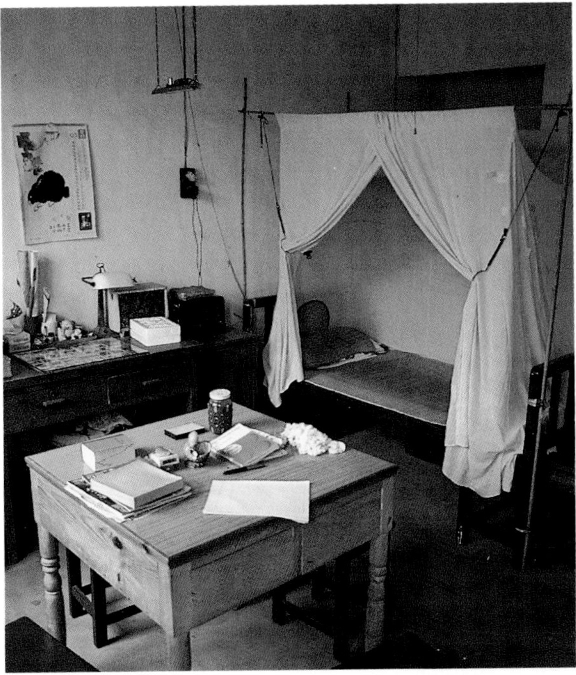

In the 1800's, the curtains around the bed were no longer needed. Houses were better built. There was not so much cold air around. Many people had separate rooms to sleep in. Then, coiled wire springs were put under the bed mattress. These made the beds more comfortable.

## Bed Coverings

People used many different covers for their beds. At first, furs were used. In Europe about 500 years ago, some people started to use sheets and pillowcases for their beds. These were often made of a cloth called **linen**. In some places, feathers were stuffed into large cloth bags to make warm bed coverings, or quilts. Blankets were made of woven wool, and they were often made at home.

Bedspreads and quilts were made of padded cotton, linen, or silk. Sometimes, they were made from patchwork. The designs were often of birds, flowers, and animals. Patchwork quilts have been made in many countries. Some very fine quilts were made in New England. A young woman might make up to fourteen quilts before she got married. The patterns on the quilts were supposed to bring happiness and good luck.

# Bathrooms and Lavatories

Until the 1900's, very few houses had baths and bathrooms. Most people washed in a bowl or a large tub. When they wanted to take a bath, they had to fill the tub with jugs of hot water. Toilets or lavatories were often outside.

▼ The Roman baths in the city of Bath in England, were built where hot springs came out of the ground. After the Roman Empire the baths were not used for a long time. Bathing in the hot springs became popular again in the 1700's.

## Baths

In ancient Greece and Rome, peop
washed themselves very often. The
cities had public lavatories an
baths. They had flushing water an
sewers. These public baths were like
health club today. There was a gym,
sauna, and a swimming pool all in on
building. People met there. They washe
in warm water and sat in hot, steam
rooms. They exercised, and the
discussed business. Then, they coole
off with a plunge into a pool of col
water. Going to the baths was a socia
occasion.

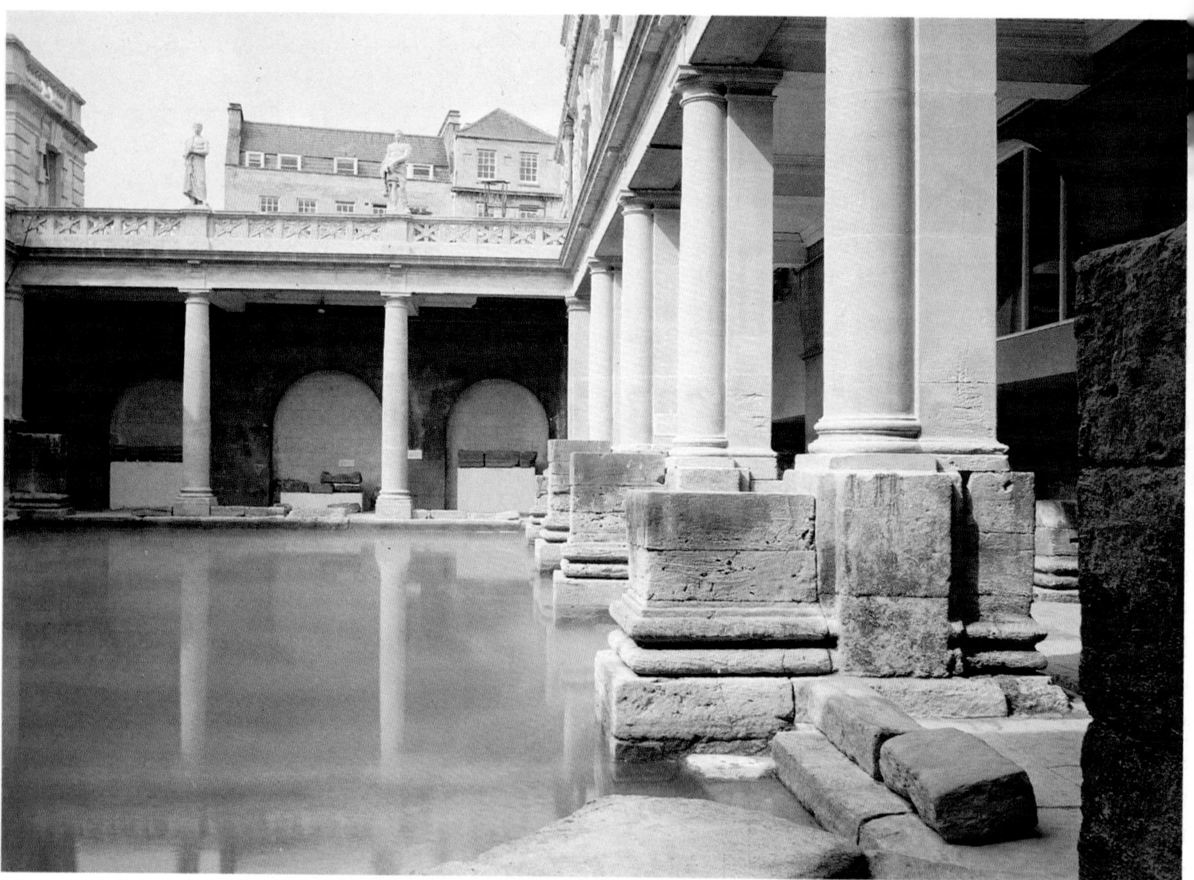

People began to think that public athing was unhealthy. Public baths ere no longer used. People washed in ieir own homes.

Early bathtubs came in all shapes and izes. The "slipper" bath looked exactly ke a large slipper. A flap lifted so that a erson could get in. The baths had to be lled with water by hand. In the 1850's, eople heated the cold water in a bath by ghting a gas fire underneath it. The first iped hot water was stored in a tank that ept it warm.

▲ In the past, there were no hot water faucets. Water had to be heated and put in the bathtub. This means it was best to share bath water, or to take small baths. Hip baths and slipper baths were smaller than the bathtubs we use today.

## Lavatories

The Romans built public lavatories. The next lavatories that we know about were in castles. They were called "garderobes." They were built into an outer wall. The waste fell down a hole to the ground below.

In the 1500's, Sir John Harrington invented a way of removing waste matter. Water flowed from a tank to a **water closet**. It flushed away waste. Queen Elizabeth I of England had one in her palace at Richmond.

Most people did not have water closets. They used pots and chairs with the pots hidden under the seat. The seat lifted up like a lid. These chairs were called **commodes**. If you could afford it, you paid the "night soil" man to take your sewage away. If not, the refuse and sewage were thrown outside. They piled up in the gutters and courtyards. This spread disease.

▲ This is a water closet or toilet made in 1887. Water was held in the tank above the pedestal. People pulled the chain to make it flush. The water and waste went out through a pipe.

# Gardens

Long ago, the Egyptians made walled gardens. They grew fig trees and grape vines, vegetables, and flowers. They made pools beside the Nile River. Blue lotus flowers grew in them.

Two thousand years ago, there were gardens on the walls of Babylon. The King of Babylon, Nebuchadnezzar, built the gardens for his wife. The gardens were in steps, or **terraces**. They were said to be one of the wonders of the world. They were called the Hanging Gardens of Babylon.

Often, Greek and Roman houses had inner courtyards. People could sit there and enjoy the shade. There was a fountain in the middle of the courtyard. There were statues and pots of flowers.

## Plants for Gardens

In the 1200's, Marco Polo visite China. There, he saw gardens whic were full of beautiful flowers. Many c these flowers, such as lilies and peonie were not brought to Europe until th 1700's.

Green plants, called **herbs**, are grow to flavor food and to make medicines. I the 1500's, herbs were planted i patterns. Little hedges divided u groups of plants. This was called a **kno garden**. Many people still use herbs i cooking. Some people know how t make medicines from herbs.

▼ These gardens are at Powys Castle in Wales. They are built at different levels to make terraces. Many plants are grown against or over the walls like the Hanging Gardens of ancient Babylon. Statues and paths were used to make the gardens more interesting.

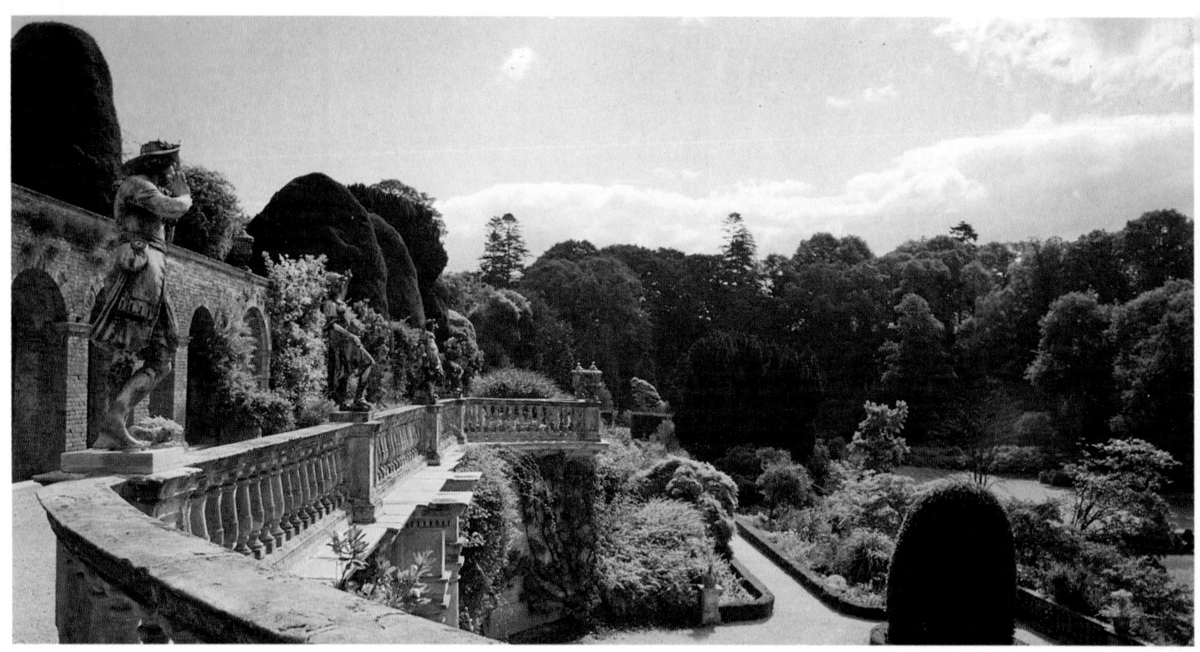

## heltered Gardens

Courtyard gardens were common in ot, dry countries. The walls gave shelter rom the sun and the wind. Often, these ourtyards had a fountain or a pool of vater. The Chinese built gardens with valls on all sides. They were quiet places o think. Some of these gardens were nade a long time ago. The gardens of uchow can still be seen today.

In Japan, gardens were made around emples. Some temple gardens were nade in the 1100's. They still exist. Some iave many types of moss plants. Others ire made up of small stones.

▲ This garden is in Granada in Spain. Spain was once ruled by Arab people from North Africa. The Arabs built many fine palaces and gardens. Small canals often ran through the middle of the gardens. Walled gardens are still built in hot countries today.

## Cottage Gardens

In Europe, country people grew their own fruit and vegetables near their homes. Sometimes, flowers were grown among the fruit and vegetables. Garden pests liked to eat the flowers better than the food plants. This mixing of plants is called "cottage-style" gardening.

▲ Country people grew fruit and vegetables to last through the winter. They also grew flowers because they looked pretty. The gardens were very simple. Cottage gardens like these are found in many parts of England today.

## The English Garden

For many years in Europe, gardens were made according to a strict pattern. They had paved paths around neat flower beds. In the 1700's, there was a new style of garden. The big gardens around country homes were arranged to look like natural countryside. Lawns, trees, and shrubs were planted to look like they had grown wild.

# Quiz

How much can you remember? Try to do this quiz. Use the glossary and the index to help you find the answers.

**1.** Here are some types of beds with the letters scrambled. Unscramble these letters to find the correct words.

a) UHOCC, b) KOMAMCH, c) TLENRUD, d) ROFURESTOP

**2.** Where
a) did people live in tepees?
b) was the sash window invented?
c) was wallpaper first used?
d) was the earliest lock used?
e) was central heating first used?

**3.** Match the descriptions (a) to (f) with the words (1) to (6) below them.

a) A roof made of straw, reeds, turf, or grass
b) A very tall building
c) A small gate set in a bigger one
d) Used to squeeze water from wet clothes
e) A person who designs and plans houses
f) A large lamp lit by candles

1) skyscraper
2) chandelier
3) mangle
4) architect
5) thatch
6) wicket

**4.** Who
a) made the first refrigerator?
b) studied Roman buildings and became a famous architect?
c) invented the lock with the notched key?
d) invented the elevator?

**5.** What
a) are porches?
b) are combination locks?
c) is linoleum?
d) is a flue?
e) are hammocks?

**6.** Complete the following sentences with a), b), c), or d).

1) People who travel in search of food are called
a) landers.
b) sweeps.
c) nomads.
d) commodes.

2) Woven cloth pictures hung on walls were called
a) posters.
b) thermostats.
c) tapestries.
d) tablecloths.

3) A metal pole used for roasting meat is
a) peat.
b) a spiral.
c) lead.
d) a spit.

4) The pictures on Roman floors made from small pieces of marble are called.
a) mosaics.
b) cauldrons.
c) solars.
d) quilts.

5) Travois were
a) kings in Europe.
b) wooden frames dragged by horses or dogs.

c) building skills.
d) a horse-drawn cart.

6) Guilds are
a) a type of money used in Holland.
b) water plants used for building.
c) apartment houses.
d) groups of crafts people.

**7.** Are these statements true or false?
a) Cement stays hard under water.
b) Slipper baths were shaped like slippers.
c) The first carpets came to Europe from North America between the 1300's and 1500's.
d) A meat safe is where butchers keep their money.
e) Knives were used long before forks.

**8.** Put the following events in order.
a) In Europe, towns were built with walls around the outside.
b) Carpetmaking began in the United States.
c) People learned to grow crops and keep animals in herds.
d) Whole walls were made of plate glass.
e) People in Europe began to copy designs used on Chinese wallpaper.

**9.** Which item does not belong in each group? Why?
a) slate, shingle, quarry, straw
b) tent, wagon, canal, barge
c) wood, coal, flue, peat
d) aqueduct, jug, cauldron, trestle
e) parlor, salon, shingles, solar

**10.** Here are ten words written backwards. Which five are names of building materials?
a) RETSASID, b) OOBMAB, c) SDAMON,
d) SEDIH, e) ENOTS, f) STRESED,
g) ROLRAP, h) DUM, i) SKCIRB,
j) SNEVO

## Answers

**1.** a) COUCH, b) HAMMOCK, c) TRUNDLE, d) FOUR POSTER

**2.** a) North America, b) England, c) China, d) Egypt e) Rome

**3.** (a) 5, (b) 1, (c) 6, (d) 3, (e) 4, (f) 2

**4.** a) Jacob Perkins, b) Andrea Palladio, c) Jeremiah Chubb d) Elisha Graves Otis

**5.** a) roofs over doorways held up by pillars
b) locks which could be opened at certain times by the right series of numbers
c) a floor covering
d) a small chimney
e) beds of cloth tied between posts

**6.** (1) c, (2) c, (3) d, (4) a, (5) b, (6) d

**7.** (a) true, (b) true, (c) false, (d) false, (e) true

**8.** (c), (a), (e), (b), (d)

**9.** a) quarry (all the others are roofing materials)
b) canal (all the others are moveable homes)
c) flue (all the others are fuel)
d) trestle (all the others can hold water)
e) shingles (all the others are types of living rooms)

**10.** b) BAMBOO, d) HIDES, e) STONE, h) MUD, i) BRICKS

# Glossary

**aqueduct:** a pipe or channel built to carry water across a valley or through a tunnel.
**architect:** a person who designs buildings and draws the plans for builders to follow.

**bamboo:** a very tall type of grass with a hard hollow stem. Bamboo can grow up to 130 feet high. It is found in hot tropical climates.
**barge:** a wide flat-bottomed boat. Barges are used for carrying goods.
**black lead:** a black mineral called plumbago. It can be used to polish metal or make pencils.
**bolt:** a bar made of wood or metal which slides across the door and frame to fasten the door shut.
**bronze:** a metal made of copper and tin.

**carbon:** an important chemical found in fuels, foods, and all living things on earth.
**castle:** a large walled fort. A nobleman lived there with his family and soldiers to fight off enemies.
**cauldron:** a large kettle or pot for boiling in. It is hung over a fire.
**cesspool:** a large underground hole which is used to collect waste drainage from a house.
**chandelier:** a large frame with branches for holding candles or light bulbs. It hangs from the ceiling.
**cholera:** a disease which gives people very bad diarrhrea and vomiting. Cholera is spread by unclean water and food, and it is easily caught.
**cistern:** a tank or reservoir for holding water.
**combination lock:** a type of lock which uses several connected actions instead of a key. The correct actions must be followed in the right order before the lock can be opened.
**commode:** a chair with a deep seat which holds a chamber pot. The pot is hidden under a lid.
**conduit:** a pipe or channel that carries water or other liquids.
**craft:** work that requires skill and must be studied and learned. Carpentry is a craft.

**dolly:** a wooden stick with arms at one end, used for stirring clothes in a washing tub.

**felt:** a kind of thick cloth made by pressing hair or wool flat.
**flue:** a pipe which carries smoke, hot air, or gases to the outside of a building.
**four-poster bed:** a large bed with one upright post at each corner. Curtains are often hung between these posts.
**furnace:** a closed chamber in which things can be heated to a very high temperature.

**gallery:** a covered walkway or passage. Galleries are often built above the ground floor and open at one side to overlook a room below.
**germ:** a tiny living thing that can cause diseases. Germs can be seen only with a very strong microscope.
**guild:** a society set up to help and support groups of workers with similar skills.
**gutter:** a channel or drain at the edge of a roof or a street. A gutter carries away rain water.
**gypsies:** groups of people who prefer to travel around rather than settle down in one spot.

**hammock:** a cloth or net hung up by cords at each end. It is used as a bed.
**herb:** plants used for medicine or to add flavor to food.
**hill fort:** a group of buildings which have a wall around them and are built on a hilltop.
**hinge:** a joint which allows one thing to swing on another.

**knot garden:** a patch of garden divided by stones or hedges where herbs can be grown.

**larder:** a small room or cupboard, with a screened air hole, where food can be kept cool and fresh.
**latch:** a bar which fastens a door or gate shut. A latch is attached to the door at one end, and the free end is lifted by a lever or handle.
**linen:** a fine, smooth cloth made from flax.
**linoleum:** a strong floor covering made by treating a fabric with a mixture of linseed oil, resins, and cork.

**mangle:** a machine with two rollers used for pressing and draining water from clothes.
**meat safe:** a container for storing meat. The safe has fine air holes to protect the meat from flies.

**osaic:** a pattern, or picture which is made by ting together small pieces of colored stone.

**mad:** someone who moves from place to ace in search of food or to find grassland for imals.

**tch:** a slight cut or nick in a hard surface.

**raffin:** a waxy liquid made from oil. It is used a fuel.

**rlor:** a small sitting room. Usually, it was nply furnished and private.

**at:** partly-rotted plants in wet marshland. at is soft and spongy to touch, but it can be ied out and used as a fuel.

**an:** a drawing to show the details of mething such as a building.

**aster:** a mixture of lime and sand made into a ste with water. It is used to coat walls or ilings. It gets hard and feels smooth to touch.

**ate glass:** strong glass which is made in large eets. Often, plate glass is used for large mirrors d windows in stores and offices.

**rch:** the part of a building which covers or otects the outer doorway.

**iarry:** a place where rocks are cut or dug from e ground.

**nge:** a large flat-topped kitchen stove. It is ade of metal and contains a fire which heats the en and hot plates.

**frigerator:** a cabinet-like machine which eps air at a low temperature.

**sh:** a tall grass-like plant with slim, strong alks. It grows in wet places.

**lon:** a large room found in big houses or laces where people can gather to sit and talk.

**ltcellar:** a container that holds salt for use on e table.

**sh:** a sliding frame which holds window ass. It is balanced by weights which allow ovement up and down.

**wage:** the waste matter which is carried away water from buildings.

**ingle:** a wooden slab used as a tile for roofs id outside walls.

**ate:** a fine-grained rock which splits easily into in, flat, smooth plates. It is used for roofing.

**solar:** a room positioned so that it catches sunlight.

**solar heating:** a way of using energy from the sun's rays to heat houses.

**spiral:** a shape or line that curves around and around while moving away from a point.

**spit:** a pointed stick on which food can be stuck and then turned over flames to be cooked.

**spring lock:** a door fastening which contains a spring that is released when touched by a key.

**story:** the part of a building which is on a particular level or floor. Some buildings have several stories built one on top of the other.

**tapestry:** a fabric in which colored threads are stitched or woven to form pictures or patterns. Tapestries covered walls and furniture.

**tepee:** a Native American's tent made from hides or cloth. It is stretched over a frame, shaped like a cone, made of poles.

**terrace:** a flat piece of ground cut into a slope like a large step.

**thatch:** a thick and waterproof roof made from layers of straw, rushes, or palm-leaves.

**travois:** a pair of trailing poles attached to each side of a horse's saddle. They are joined by a piece of cloth, and used to carry people and belongings.

**trestle:** a wooden or metal crisscross framework that supports a flat surface such as a table.

**trundle bed:** a type of bed on low wheels which can be pushed under a larger bed.

**typhoid fever:** a serious disease which causes a high temperature, red spots, and stomach pains. It is spread by unclean food and water.

**upholstery:** the springs, padding, stuffing, and covers which are fitted over a frame. Upholstery makes chairs and sofas more comfortable.

**water closet:** a lavatory where the waste is carried off by water to a drain.

**wick:** the twisted threads of cotton or another substance which draws up oil or grease to the flame of a candle or lamp.

**wicket:** a small door in or near a larger gate.

**withdrawing room:** a comfortably furnished sitting room. In the past, people used to meet there after their meals.

# Index